YOUR LIVING Legacy

A Personal Journal of Remembrances to Guide Loved Ones

Susan Fielder Mears

Contemporary Books

Library of Congress Cataloging-in-Publication Data

Mears, Susan Fielder.
    Your living legacy : a personal journey of remembrances to guide loved ones / Susan Fielder Mears.
       p.   cm.
    ISBN 0-8092-2905-6 (pbk.)
    1. Death—Psychological aspects—Miscellanea.   2. Autobiography—Authorship—Miscellanea.   3. Estate planning—Miscellanea.   I. Title.
BF789.D4M38   1998
155.9′37—dc21
                                                                                                98-13270
                                                                                                    CIP

Cover design by Monica Baziuk
Cover and interior photography by Sharon Hoogstraten (except pages 1, 2, 101, 102, 119, 120, 160, and 164)

Published by Contemporary Books
A division of NTC/Contemporary Publishing Group, Inc.
4255 West Touhy Avenue, Lincolnwood (Chicago), Illinois 60646-1975 U.S.A.
Copyright © 1998 by Susan Fielder Mears
All rights reserved. No part of this book may be reproduced, stored in a retrieval system, or transmitted in any form or by any means, electronic, mechanical, photocopying, recording, or otherwise, without the prior permission of NTC/Contemporary Publishing Group, Inc.
Printed in the United States of America
International Standard Book Number: 0-8092-2905-6
18 17 16 15 14 13 12 11 10 9 8 7 6 5 4 3 2 1

*This book has been created with a great deal of care
and thought to provide a place to record one's life,
personal feelings, memories, and wishes for the
ultimate distribution of personal belongings.
This document is not binding and the user is urged
to maintain a legal Will or Living Trust
and consider the wishes contained herein as a
personal supplement to guide one's executor and heirs.*

If you were to die tomorrow,

would your Will provide your family and friends
with all of the information they would want and need?
If not, imagine how their loss would be compounded
by having to make countless decisions and choices
without your being there to counsel them.

This informal supplement to your legal Will or Living Trust
will help you organize and communicate to family and
loved ones your personal wishes, favorite memories,
and special feelings before you are gone.

Take your time.
This can become a treasure chest of life experiences.
Write in it as you would a journal or diary, making
changes as needed. Embellish it with articles and pictures.
Whatever you make of it will be cherished
in the hearts of those you leave behind.

Everyone who comes

Knows that they must go . . .

Everyone has feelings

They know they need to show . . .

Everyone has special thoughts

That come from in their heart . . .

And here's a way to leave behind

Your legacy of art.

—Susan Fielder Mears

Contents

Foreword – ix

My Wishes – xi

I. The Tapestry of Life
Experiences That Shaped My Destiny – 1

Achievements – 4

Memorable Moments – 7

Life-Changing Events – 9

Inspirational Thoughts, Guiding Words of Advice & Wisdom – 11

The Faith Factor – 13

It Was So Romantic – 15

Secrets – 17

Great Adventures – 19

Favorite Travels – 21

Small-World Stories – 23

Favorite Books, Movies & Plays – 25

Poems & Quotes – 27

Recipes I Made Famous – 29

Drawings – 31

Games & Hobbies – 33

My Life Story – 35

II. When I Couldn't Find the Words
Special Notes to & About Others – 39

III. You Can't Take It with You
Distribution of My Worldly Possessions – 65

Remember Me by These Special Things – 68

My Pet & Loyal Companion – 95

IV. The Long Road Home

My Family History - 101

Historical Family Stories - 104
Your Immediate Family Tree - 109
Your Extended Family Tree - 110
Your Ancestors' Family Tree - 111
Family Medical History - 112
Location of Family Memorabilia - 114

V. Exit Dancing

My Final Arrangements - 119

Funeral-Memorial Arrangements - 123
Other Arrangements - 126
Vital Statistics - 128
Professional Advisors - 129
For Your Information - 131

VI. Practical Issues

Getting Organized - 139

Record of Important Documents, Etc. - 142
Insurance Records - 146
Other Items/Documents - 147
Your Will - 148
Your Executor - 150
Your Living Will - 151
Organ Donation - 152
Social Security Benefits - 153
Veterans Benefits - 154
Personal Thoughts & Reflections - 155

Sands of Time - 159

Foreword

I came upon this project out of pain and grief, but mostly out of necessity. While everyone is eager for the celebration surrounding the birth of a new life, it is with trepidation and procrastination we prepare for death. Tomorrow seems a perfect choice for dispersing what has taken a lifetime to accumulate. My mother had planned on living forever, it seemed, and then a wild card took us by surprise, and in a matter of weeks she was gone. In a bedroom drawer I discovered a simpler version of this book, one that I had given her three years earlier. The pages were a blank, pristine white, like clean sheets on a freshly made bed, unmarred by a restless sleeper. It lay empty, much like our bodies do without a spirit. I could only imagine what secrets had never been written, what wishes had never been shared.

Truly you cannot judge a book by its cover, for a book is nothing at all without its contents. I was left in the wake of my mother's leaving to struggle with my brothers over details and deadlines, caught between fairness and futility. Nothing in this world truly belongs to us; rather we are entrusted as caretakers, shepherds in the field of life. My hope is that the anguish of others will be diminished through the use of this journal. So, I encourage you to take the time to fill this out, while the sun is still high in the sky, and leave a legacy to comfort your loved ones in the days and weeks after your death. On these pages you can provide answers to the many questions that remain once you are gone. On these pages you can make sure you will not be forgotten.

—Susan Fielder Mears

My Wishes

Within this book, I have gathered my special thoughts, memories, and requests, which I am leaving for my family and friends. It contains personal recollections, feelings about my life, and my requests for distribution of certain belongings.

I recognize that this is not a legal supplement of my Will or Living Trust; however, any requests herein are expressed in good faith to my executor in the hope that they will be honored. Above all, I trust that my loved ones will enjoy this personal perspective of my life and be assured of my fondest farewell wishes.

Signed, *Patricia Mabanag Martinez Olson*

on the *1ST* day of *October* in the year *1998*

I entrust this book to *Olympia Aruna Eurasia Martinez*

Address _____

Phone _____ Relationship *The first daughter*

In the event this guardian is someone other than my executor, I hope that my executor will honor my wishes to utilize the person named above as my chosen spokesperson for the requests outlined herein.

In case the above person is not able to carry out my wishes at the time of my death,

I choose _____ as an alternate.

Address _____

Phone _____ Relationship _____

Chapter I

The Tapestry of Life
Experiences That Shaped My Destiny

Our lives are finely woven and richly textured, echoing the events and relationships that cross our paths. Prized trophies, framed diplomas, baby shoes, and wedding albums—these are reminders of the experiences that shaped our destiny. What was once an obstacle becomes a stepping stone. Many times we choose to participate, but ultimately our destiny is held in the hands of the Master Sculptor as our lives are invisibly shaped. Whether by accident or divine appointment, we arrive at places we never could have dreamed, endured hardships we never could have imagined, and come out on the other side of the storm a better person. For some life is navigated with precision, while others drive kamikaze-style into the night with empty pockets and a tank full of dreams, willing to go wherever the road leads. With inspired direction or reckless abandon, we run after the magic of living, its fine nuances and subtle opportunities rising and falling into a crescendo of possibility. These golden threads highlight our existence in the tapestry called life, forever changing their lyrical pattern as lives intertwine.

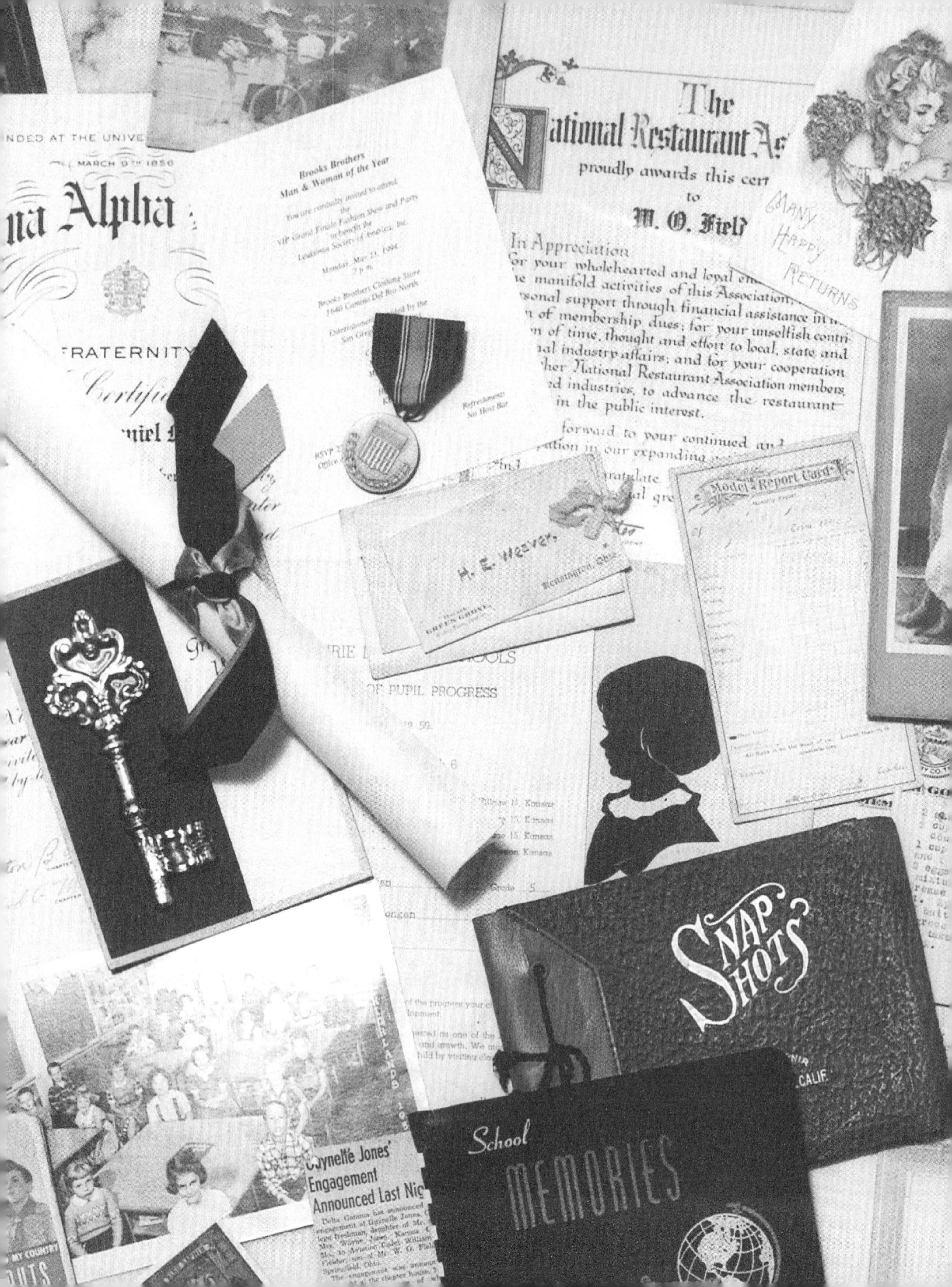

MARCH 9TH 1856
FRATERNITY
Brooks Brothers
Man & Woman of the Year
Refreshments
No Host Bar
proudly awards this
to
In Appreciation
MANY HAPPY RETURNS
Model Report Card
H. E. Weaver
Kensington, Ohio
GREEN GROVE
OF PUPIL PROGRESS
SNAP SHOTS
Engagement
Announced Last
School
MEMORIES
MY COUNTRY

The Tapestry of Life

An individual's life

becomes intricately sculpted over time

through an accumulation of diverse elements: guiding philosophies,

seemingly insignificant incidents, enjoyable pastimes or hobbies,

favorite foods, adventuresome travels, and beloved poems, books, and

music. Many times the circumstances that shape our lives

are unknown or eventually forgotten by others.

The following pages prompt you to record those things that move you,

bring a smile to your face, or encourage you through one of life's storms.

You may wish to attach newspaper articles, recipes, pictures,

printed poems, or other items to which you often refer.

Achievements

*Housewife or President of the company,
whatever has made you proud deserves a journal entry.*

_____
_____
_____
_____
_____
_____
_____
_____
_____
_____
_____
_____
_____
_____
_____
_____
_____
_____
_____

The Tapestry of Life

Your Living Legacy

The Tapestry of Life

Memorable Moments

*Everybody has them. You know what yours are.
Leave them behind for others to share.*

_____
_____
_____
_____
_____
_____
_____
_____
_____
_____
_____
_____
_____
_____
_____
_____
_____
_____
_____
_____
_____

Your Living Legacy

Life-Changing Events

Was it Fate, Planned, or Chance? Whether they were hard work or good fortune, share the experiences that shifted your destiny.

_____
_____
_____
_____
_____
_____
_____
_____
_____
_____
_____
_____
_____
_____
_____
_____
_____
_____
_____
_____
_____
_____
_____
_____
_____

The Tapestry of Life

Inspirational Thoughts, Guiding Words of Advice & Wisdom

Record the famous last words, notable quotes, or philosophies that steered your life's course.

The Faith Factor

Share your spiritual experiences and beliefs.

It Was So Romantic

A starry night, a stolen kiss—please tell us now, it was such bliss!

Your Living Legacy

Secrets

You promised you'd never tell . . . well, here's your chance!

_____
_____
_____
_____
_____
_____
_____
_____
_____
_____
_____
_____
_____
_____
_____
_____
_____
_____
_____
_____
_____
_____

Great Adventures

What exciting escapades can you share?

Favorite Travels

Pack a bag; get a map! Tell where you've been and whom you've met!

Your Living Legacy

Small-World Stories

Around the block, across the country, or halfway around the globe, chance meetings make it a small world.

Favorite Books, Movies & Plays

*Encore! Encore! Whether you read it, watched it,
or applauded it, share your favorites and the reasons why.*

_____
_____
_____
_____
_____
_____
_____
_____
_____
_____
_____
_____
_____
_____
_____
_____
_____
_____
_____
_____

Poems & Quotes

I hate the guys who criticize

and minimize the other guys

whose enterprise has made them rise

above the guys who criticize.

—Author Unknown

Recipes I Made Famous

Recipe for Eating Crow

Buy one extra large crow, making sure it is tough and difficult to swallow.
Marinate overnight with remorse.
Sprinkle generously with sincere apologies and bake at a high temperature.
Stew frequently in your own juices until very uncomfortable.
Serve quickly and garnish with a fresh request for forgiveness.

Now add your real recipes!

_____
_____
_____
_____
_____
_____
_____
_____
_____
_____
_____
_____
_____
_____

The Tapestry of Life

Drawings

A picture is worth a thousand words.

The Tapestry of Life

Games & Hobbies

Win or lose, it's how you played!
Name your game, collectible, or favorite pastime.

My Life Story

Your Living Legacy

The Tapestry of Life

Your Living Legacy

Chapter II

When I Couldn't Find the Words
Special Notes to & About Others

In the electronic age of television and video, tape recorders and answering machines, the written word has taken a backseat to the ease of reaching for the cool plastic of the telephone receiver. But often we leave the most important things unsaid, swept away in an ocean of mundane day-to-day activities. These private memories will live on long after we are gone, to comfort our loved ones in a tangible way, to be read and remembered. More important than leaving behind financial security and belongings is leaving behind your spirit, your voice, your connection to others, a bridge that can touch the living in the gap left behind after death.

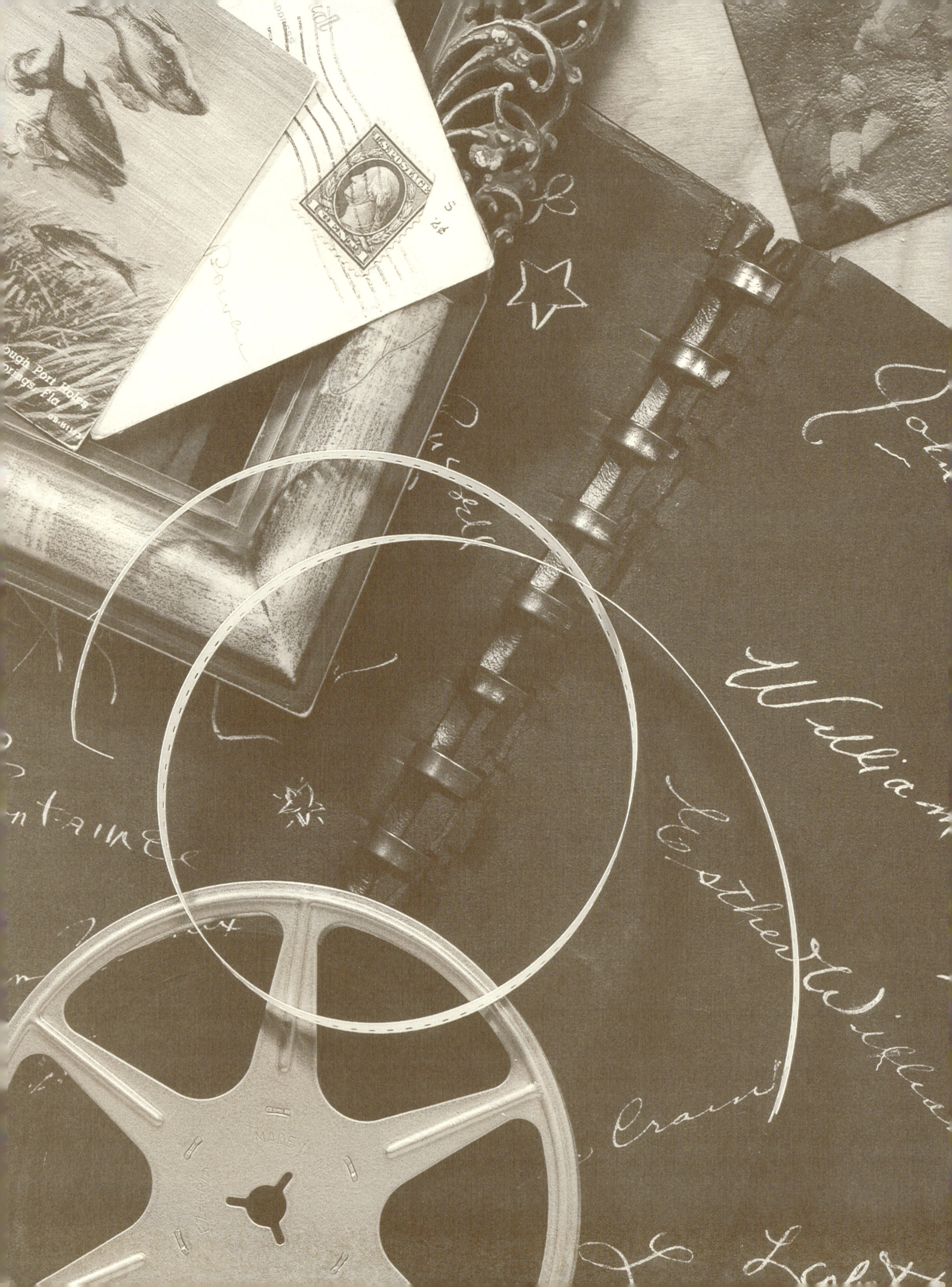
William

When I Couldn't Find the Words

Imagine for a moment

*the conversation you would want to share
with a loved one, knowing that you had only a few hours left together,
and simply begin writing down or taping the thoughts that come to mind.
You may convey your message in letter form, capture it on a tape recorder,
or treat it as a diary passage, dating each entry as you record it.
If any unresolved issues linger in your personal relationships,
now is the time to put them to rest.*

*We all have special people who have influenced
the course of our life and helped create who we are.
Below is a list that will help stimulate your memory.*

Spouse	*Cousins*	*Friends*
Children	*Nieces*	*Teachers*
Parents	*Nephews*	*Counselors*
Siblings	*In-Laws*	*Mentors*
Grandparents	*Stepparents*	*Religious Leaders*
Aunts	*Stepchildren*	*Associates*
Uncles	*Other Family*	*Heroes*

A Special Note To

When I Couldn't Find the Words

A Special Note To

_____

Your Living Legacy

A Special Note To

_____

A Special Note To

Your Living Legacy

A Special Note To

_____

When I Couldn't Find the Words

A Special Note To

A Special Note To

_____

A Special Note To

A Special Note To

When I Couldn't Find the Words

A Special Note To

_____

A Special Note To

_____

A Special Note To

_____

A Special Note To

_____

When I Couldn't Find the Words

A Special Note To

_____

A Special Note To

When I Couldn't Find the Words

A Special Note To

_____

_____
_____
_____
_____
_____
_____
_____
_____
_____
_____
_____
_____
_____
_____
_____
_____
_____
_____
_____
_____
_____
_____
_____
_____

Your Living Legacy

A Special Note To

_____

When I Couldn't Find the Words

A Special Note To

_____

A Special Note To

A Special Note To

Personal Notes

When I Couldn't Find the Words

Your Living Legacy

Chapter III

You Can't Take It with You
Distribution of My Worldly Possessions

I know a woman who has what she calls the "handbag theory" of life. It's a simple one, she claims, because we have a tendency to complicate things that would happen naturally. Her theory is this: no matter how large or how small a purse you carry, it always ends up full—with enough room for what you need to get by, and then some. And while it's true a larger handbag will hold more things, many times they are difficult to find. Now with a smaller purse, you've got less to look after, and it's a whole lot easier to carry. The same holds true for living. It seems ironic that we leave this world about the same as when we came in, hopefully no worse for the wear, only we have accumulated some stuff along the way. So, whether you have a lot or a little, she says, choose carefully what you do with it, and divine providence will take care of the rest. Because, after all, you can't take it with you; you can only enjoy it while you're here.

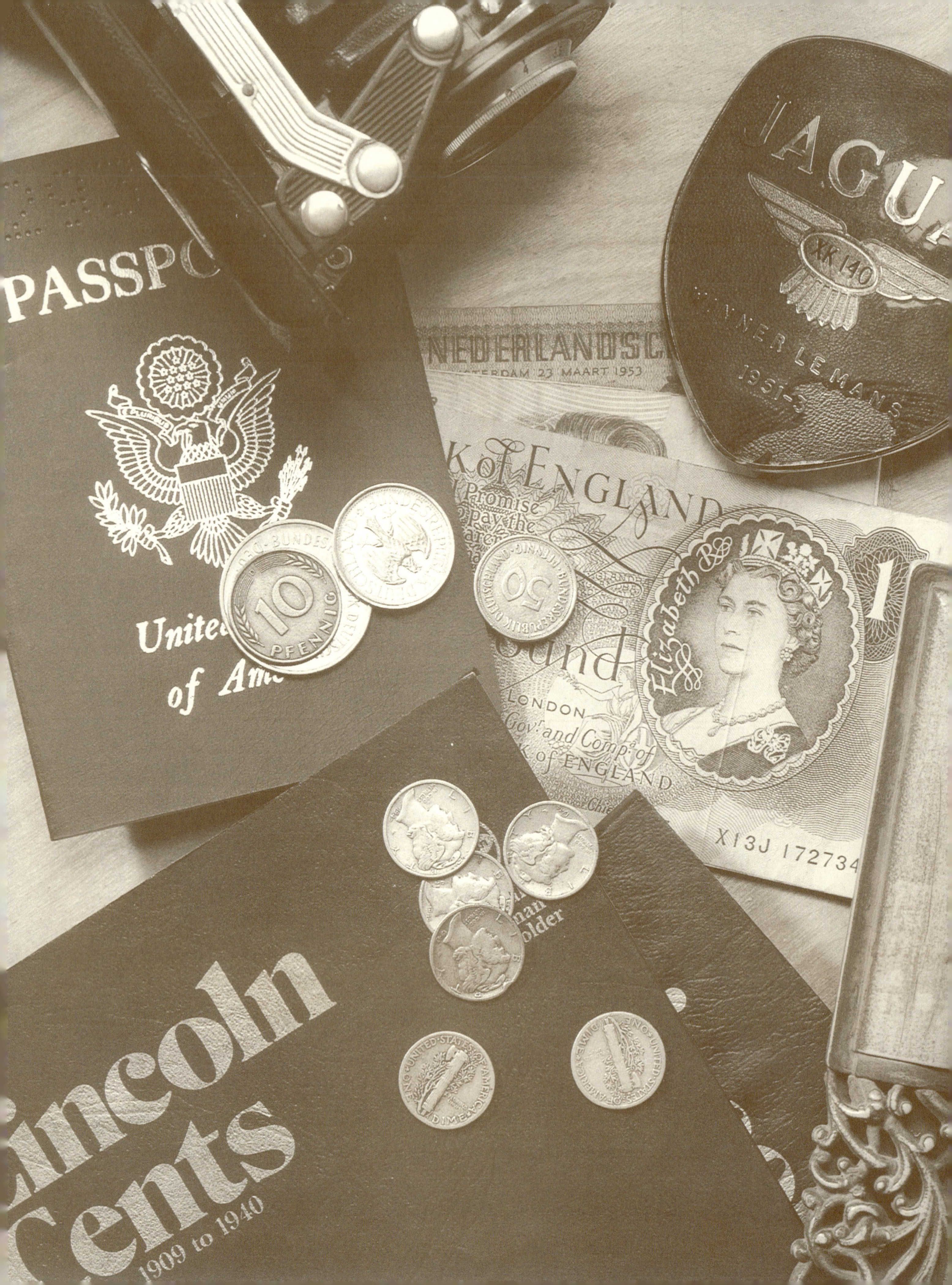
PASSPO
Unite
of Am
10
PFENNIG
NEDERLANDSC
TERDAM 23 MAART 1953
K of ENGLAND
Promise
pay the
50
LONDON
Gov. and Comp. of
of ENGLAND
Elizabeth
X13J 172734
AGU
XK 140
1951-3
incoln
Cents
1909 to 1940
DIME

You Can't Take It with You

What you decide here

*regarding your possessions and their distribution
can help keep peace within your family and preserve your keepsakes
in a very special and thoughtful way. The fill-in-the-blank format
allows you to date and change entries whenever you wish.*

*Even close families can succumb to hurt feelings, misunderstandings,
or estrangement when it comes time to distribute personal belongings.
The "It won't matter when I'm gone" mindset is a bitter legacy to
leave your loved ones, especially if they were promised something
in confidence before your death. Remember, though, distributions must
necessarily abide by the legal process as directed by your executor.*

*Below is a list to guide you in cataloging your possessions.
Choose the appropriate categories and itemize on the following pages.*

Jewelry	Art	Books
Furs	Antiques/Collectibles	Music & Videos
Clothes	Furniture	Computers/Software
Accessories	Appliances	Electronics
Silver	Scrapbooks	Tools
Crystal	Photo Albums	Sports Equipment
China	Holiday Decorations	Vehicles
Linens	Diaries	Other

Remember Me by These Special Things

My wishes are for the distribution of my personal belongings as follows. At the time of my death, if any item is not in my estate, then the gifts shall lapse. If any beneficiary has died, then the gifts shall be either distributed in accordance with the terms of my Will or I shall have designated alternates, herein.

_____
(category)

Item(s) _____ Date _____

Description and/or History _____

_____ Location _____

Is Bequeathed to _____ Alternate _____

Item(s) _____ Date _____

Description and/or History _____

_____ Location _____

Is Bequeathed to _____ Alternate _____

Item(s) _____ Date _____

Description and/or History _____

_____ Location _____

Is Bequeathed to _____ Alternate _____

_____
(category)

Item(s) _____ Date _____

Description and/or History _____

_____ Location _____

Is Bequeathed to _____ Alternate _____

Item(s) _____ Date _____

Description and/or History _____

_____ Location _____

Is Bequeathed to _____ Alternate _____

Item(s) _____ Date _____

Description and/or History _____

_____ Location _____

Is Bequeathed to _____ Alternate _____

Item(s) _____ Date _____

Description and/or History _____

_____ Location _____

Is Bequeathed to _____ Alternate _____

_____
(category)

Item(s) _____ Date _____

Description and/or History _____

_____ Location _____

Is Bequeathed to _____ Alternate _____

Item(s) _____ Date _____

Description and/or History _____

_____ Location _____

Is Bequeathed to _____ Alternate _____

Item(s) _____ Date _____

Description and/or History _____

_____ Location _____

Is Bequeathed to _____ Alternate _____

Item(s) _____ Date _____

Description and/or History _____

_____ Location _____

Is Bequeathed to _____ Alternate _____

You Can't Take It with You

_____
(category)

Item(s) _____ Date _____

Description and/or History _____

_____ Location _____

Is Bequeathed to _____ Alternate _____

Item(s) _____ Date _____

Description and/or History _____

_____ Location _____

Is Bequeathed to _____ Alternate _____

Item(s) _____ Date _____

Description and/or History _____

_____ Location _____

Is Bequeathed to _____ Alternate _____

Item(s) _____ Date _____

Description and/or History _____

_____ Location _____

Is Bequeathed to _____ Alternate _____

Your Living Legacy

_____
(category)

Item(s) _____ Date _____

Description and/or History _____

_____ Location _____

Is Bequeathed to _____ Alternate _____

Item(s) _____ Date _____

Description and/or History _____

_____ Location _____

Is Bequeathed to _____ Alternate _____

Item(s) _____ Date _____

Description and/or History _____

_____ Location _____

Is Bequeathed to _____ Alternate _____

Item(s) _____ Date _____

Description and/or History _____

_____ Location _____

Is Bequeathed to _____ Alternate _____

_____
(category)

Item(s) _____ Date _____

Description and/or History _____

_____ Location _____

Is Bequeathed to _____ Alternate _____

Item(s) _____ Date _____

Description and/or History _____

_____ Location _____

Is Bequeathed to _____ Alternate _____

Item(s) _____ Date _____

Description and/or History _____

_____ Location _____

Is Bequeathed to _____ Alternate _____

Item(s) _____ Date _____

Description and/or History _____

_____ Location _____

Is Bequeathed to _____ Alternate _____

Your Living Legacy

_____
(category)

Item(s) _____ Date _____

Description and/or History _____

_____ Location _____

Is Bequeathed to _____ Alternate _____

Item(s) _____ Date _____

Description and/or History _____

_____ Location _____

Is Bequeathed to _____ Alternate _____

Item(s) _____ Date _____

Description and/or History _____

_____ Location _____

Is Bequeathed to _____ Alternate _____

Item(s) _____ Date _____

Description and/or History _____

_____ Location _____

Is Bequeathed to _____ Alternate _____

You Can't Take It with You

_____
(category)

Item(s) _____ Date _____

Description and/or History _____

_____ Location _____

Is Bequeathed to _____ Alternate _____

Item(s) _____ Date _____

Description and/or History _____

_____ Location _____

Is Bequeathed to _____ Alternate _____

Item(s) _____ Date _____

Description and/or History _____

_____ Location _____

Is Bequeathed to _____ Alternate _____

Item(s) _____ Date _____

Description and/or History _____

_____ Location _____

Is Bequeathed to _____ Alternate _____

_____
(category)

Item(s) _____ Date _____

Description and/or History _____

_____ Location _____

Is Bequeathed to _____ Alternate _____

Item(s) _____ Date _____

Description and/or History _____

_____ Location _____

Is Bequeathed to _____ Alternate _____

Item(s) _____ Date _____

Description and/or History _____

_____ Location _____

Is Bequeathed to _____ Alternate _____

Item(s) _____ Date _____

Description and/or History _____

_____ Location _____

Is Bequeathed to _____ Alternate _____

You Can't Take It with You

_____
(category)

Item(s) _____ Date _____

Description and/or History _____

_____ Location _____

Is Bequeathed to _____ Alternate _____

Item(s) _____ Date _____

Description and/or History _____

_____ Location _____

Is Bequeathed to _____ Alternate _____

Item(s) _____ Date _____

Description and/or History _____

_____ Location _____

Is Bequeathed to _____ Alternate _____

Item(s) _____ Date _____

Description and/or History _____

_____ Location _____

Is Bequeathed to _____ Alternate _____

_____
(category)

Item(s) _____ Date _____

Description and/or History _____

_____ Location _____

Is Bequeathed to _____ Alternate _____

Item(s) _____ Date _____

Description and/or History _____

_____ Location _____

Is Bequeathed to _____ Alternate _____

Item(s) _____ Date _____

Description and/or History _____

_____ Location _____

Is Bequeathed to _____ Alternate _____

Item(s) _____ Date _____

Description and/or History _____

_____ Location _____

Is Bequeathed to _____ Alternate _____

_____
(category)

Item(s) _____ Date _____

Description and/or History _____

_____ Location _____

Is Bequeathed to _____ Alternate _____

Item(s) _____ Date _____

Description and/or History _____

_____ Location _____

Is Bequeathed to _____ Alternate _____

Item(s) _____ Date _____

Description and/or History _____

_____ Location _____

Is Bequeathed to _____ Alternate _____

Item(s) _____ Date _____

Description and/or History _____

_____ Location _____

Is Bequeathed to _____ Alternate _____

Your Living Legacy

_____
(category)

Item(s) _____ Date _____

Description and/or History _____

_____ Location _____

Is Bequeathed to _____ Alternate _____

Item(s) _____ Date _____

Description and/or History _____

_____ Location _____

Is Bequeathed to _____ Alternate _____

Item(s) _____ Date _____

Description and/or History _____

_____ Location _____

Is Bequeathed to _____ Alternate _____

Item(s) _____ Date _____

Description and/or History _____

_____ Location _____

Is Bequeathed to _____ Alternate _____

You Can't Take It with You

_____
(category)

Item(s) _____ Date _____

Description and/or History _____

_____ Location _____

Is Bequeathed to _____ Alternate _____

Item(s) _____ Date _____

Description and/or History _____

_____ Location _____

Is Bequeathed to _____ Alternate _____

Item(s) _____ Date _____

Description and/or History _____

_____ Location _____

Is Bequeathed to _____ Alternate _____

Item(s) _____ Date _____

Description and/or History _____

_____ Location _____

Is Bequeathed to _____ Alternate _____

_____
(category)

Item(s) _____ Date _____

Description and/or History _____

_____ Location _____

Is Bequeathed to _____ Alternate _____

Item(s) _____ Date _____

Description and/or History _____

_____ Location _____

Is Bequeathed to _____ Alternate _____

Item(s) _____ Date _____

Description and/or History _____

_____ Location _____

Is Bequeathed to _____ Alternate _____

Item(s) _____ Date _____

Description and/or History _____

_____ Location _____

Is Bequeathed to _____ Alternate _____

You Can't Take It with You

_____
(category)

Item(s) _____ Date _____

Description and/or History _____

_____ Location _____

Is Bequeathed to _____ Alternate _____

Item(s) _____ Date _____

Description and/or History _____

_____ Location _____

Is Bequeathed to _____ Alternate _____

Item(s) _____ Date _____

Description and/or History _____

_____ Location _____

Is Bequeathed to _____ Alternate _____

Item(s) _____ Date _____

Description and/or History _____

_____ Location _____

Is Bequeathed to _____ Alternate _____

Your Living Legacy

_____
(category)

Item(s) _____ Date _____

Description and/or History _____

_____ Location _____

Is Bequeathed to _____ Alternate _____

Item(s) _____ Date _____

Description and/or History _____

_____ Location _____

Is Bequeathed to _____ Alternate _____

Item(s) _____ Date _____

Description and/or History _____

_____ Location _____

Is Bequeathed to _____ Alternate _____

Item(s) _____ Date _____

Description and/or History _____

_____ Location _____

Is Bequeathed to _____ Alternate _____

_____
(category)

Item(s) _____ Date _____

Description and/or History _____

_____ Location _____

Is Bequeathed to _____ Alternate _____

Item(s) _____ Date _____

Description and/or History _____

_____ Location _____

Is Bequeathed to _____ Alternate _____

Item(s) _____ Date _____

Description and/or History _____

_____ Location _____

Is Bequeathed to _____ Alternate _____

Item(s) _____ Date _____

Description and/or History _____

_____ Location _____

Is Bequeathed to _____ Alternate _____

_____
(category)

Item(s) _____ Date _____

Description and/or History _____

_____ Location _____

Is Bequeathed to _____ Alternate _____

Item(s) _____ Date _____

Description and/or History _____

_____ Location _____

Is Bequeathed to _____ Alternate _____

Item(s) _____ Date _____

Description and/or History _____

_____ Location _____

Is Bequeathed to _____ Alternate _____

Item(s) _____ Date _____

Description and/or History _____

_____ Location _____

Is Bequeathed to _____ Alternate _____

_____
(category)

Item(s) _____ Date _____

Description and/or History _____

_____ Location _____

Is Bequeathed to _____ Alternate _____

Item(s) _____ Date _____

Description and/or History _____

_____ Location _____

Is Bequeathed to _____ Alternate _____

Item(s) _____ Date _____

Description and/or History _____

_____ Location _____

Is Bequeathed to _____ Alternate _____

Item(s) _____ Date _____

Description and/or History _____

_____ Location _____

Is Bequeathed to _____ Alternate _____

Your Living Legacy

_____
(category)

Item(s) _____ Date _____

Description and/or History _____

_____ Location _____

Is Bequeathed to _____ Alternate _____

Item(s) _____ Date _____

Description and/or History _____

_____ Location _____

Is Bequeathed to _____ Alternate _____

Item(s) _____ Date _____

Description and/or History _____

_____ Location _____

Is Bequeathed to _____ Alternate _____

Item(s) _____ Date _____

Description and/or History _____

_____ Location _____

Is Bequeathed to _____ Alternate _____

You Can't Take It with You

_____
(category)

Item(s) _____ Date _____

Description and/or History _____

_____ Location _____

Is Bequeathed to _____ Alternate _____

Item(s) _____ Date _____

Description and/or History _____

_____ Location _____

Is Bequeathed to _____ Alternate _____

Item(s) _____ Date _____

Description and/or History _____

_____ Location _____

Is Bequeathed to _____ Alternate _____

Item(s) _____ Date _____

Description and/or History _____

_____ Location _____

Is Bequeathed to _____ Alternate _____

_____
(category)

Item(s) _____ Date _____

Description and/or History _____

_____ Location _____

Is Bequeathed to _____ Alternate _____

Item(s) _____ Date _____

Description and/or History _____

_____ Location _____

Is Bequeathed to _____ Alternate _____

Item(s) _____ Date _____

Description and/or History _____

_____ Location _____

Is Bequeathed to _____ Alternate _____

Item(s) _____ Date _____

Description and/or History _____

_____ Location _____

Is Bequeathed to _____ Alternate _____

You Can't Take It with You

_____
(category)

Item(s) _____ Date _____

Description and/or History _____

_____ Location _____

Is Bequeathed to _____ Alternate _____

Item(s) _____ Date _____

Description and/or History _____

_____ Location _____

Is Bequeathed to _____ Alternate _____

Item(s) _____ Date _____

Description and/or History _____

_____ Location _____

Is Bequeathed to _____ Alternate _____

Item(s) _____ Date _____

Description and/or History _____

_____ Location _____

Is Bequeathed to _____ Alternate _____

_____
(category)

Item(s) _____ Date _____

Description and/or History _____

_____ Location _____

Is Bequeathed to _____ Alternate _____

Item(s) _____ Date _____

Description and/or History _____

_____ Location _____

Is Bequeathed to _____ Alternate _____

Item(s) _____ Date _____

Description and/or History _____

_____ Location _____

Is Bequeathed to _____ Alternate _____

Item(s) _____ Date _____

Description and/or History _____

_____ Location _____

Is Bequeathed to _____ Alternate _____

You Can't Take It with You

_____
(category)

Item(s) _____ Date _____

Description and/or History _____

_____ Location _____

Is Bequeathed to _____ Alternate _____

Item(s) _____ Date _____

Description and/or History _____

_____ Location _____

Is Bequeathed to _____ Alternate _____

Item(s) _____ Date _____

Description and/or History _____

_____ Location _____

Is Bequeathed to _____ Alternate _____

Item(s) _____ Date _____

Description and/or History _____

_____ Location _____

Is Bequeathed to _____ Alternate _____

Your Living Legacy

_____
(category)

Item(s) _____ Date _____

Description and/or History _____

_____ Location _____

Is Bequeathed to _____ Alternate _____

Item(s) _____ Date _____

Description and/or History _____

_____ Location _____

Is Bequeathed to _____ Alternate _____

Item(s) _____ Date _____

Description and/or History _____

_____ Location _____

Is Bequeathed to _____ Alternate _____

Item(s) _____ Date _____

Description and/or History _____

_____ Location _____

Is Bequeathed to _____ Alternate _____

You Can't Take It with You

My Pet & Loyal Companion

Pet's Name _____

Birthday_____

Nicknames _____

Breed _____ Registration Numbers _____

Identifying Marks _____

My Pet's Likes and Dislikes _____

Favorite Toys_____

Favorite Scratch Spot_____

Foods_____

Habits _____

Tricks_____

Medical History _____

_____

Veterinarian _____ Phone _____

Daycare _____ Phone _____

I Would Like to Leave _____
(pet's name)

In the Care of _____

Phone _____

If my selected caretaker is unable to fulfill my wish, my preferred alternates listed in order are as follows:

_____

_____

(Make sure designated person is aware of this responsibility.)

Your Living Legacy

Pet's Name _____

Birthday _____

Nicknames _____

Breed _____ Registration Numbers _____

Identifying Marks _____

My Pet's Likes and Dislikes _____

Favorite Toys _____

Favorite Scratch Spot _____

Foods _____

Habits _____

Tricks _____

Medical History _____

_____

Veterinarian _____ Phone _____

Daycare _____ Phone _____

I Would Like to Leave _____
                                  (pet's name)

In the Care of _____
Phone _____

If my selected caretaker is unable to fulfill my wish,
my preferred alternates listed in order are as follows:

_____

_____

(Make sure designated person is aware of this responsibility.)

Personal Notes

Your Living Legacy

You Can't Take It with You

Your Living Legacy

Chapter IV
The Long Road Home
My Family History

Photo albums lie in a pile, stacked and strewn haphazardly. These albums are my family and friends, my heritage, my past. Inside, though the pages are yellow and tattered, the images spring to life like the warm glow radiating from a winter fire. These memories give me pleasure, conjuring up the smell of warm pies, sweet lullabies, and wishes made on shooting stars. I remember the soft skin of my grandmother as she cradled me in her arms, a pillow of love on which I rested my head. I slept in the same bed my mother slept in as a girl, and her mother before her. I close my eyes and surround myself with the cool dank of the attic in summer, a secret hideaway of long forgotten dances and diaries, desires and disappointments, remnants of a yesterday I yearn to experience again. I feel connected, part of the universal scheme, a descendent of and an heir to the rich history of my ancestors. To anyone else, these photos are nameless faces, but to me they are my lifeblood, coursing the long road home through each generation.

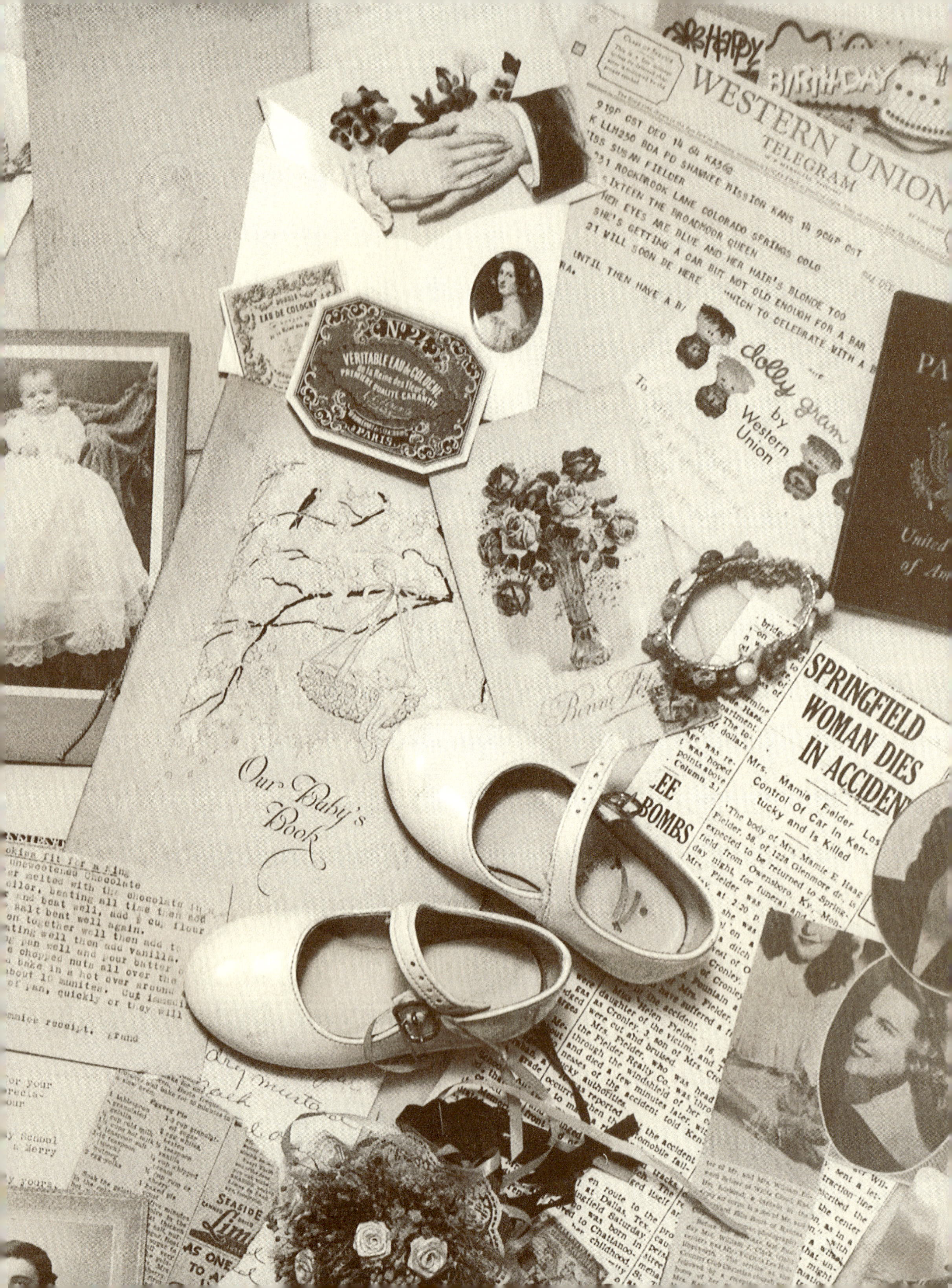
HAPPY BIRTHDAY
WESTERN UNION
TELEGRAM
SIXTEEN THE BROADMOOR QUEEN
HER EYES ARE BLUE AND HER HAIR'S BLONDE TOO
SHE'S GETTING A CAR BUT NOT OLD ENOUGH FOR A BAR
21 WILL SOON BE HERE
No 24
VERITABLE EAU de COLOGNE
PARIS
dolly gram
by
Western
Union
Our Baby's Book
SPRINGFIELD
WOMAN DIES
IN ACCIDENT
Mrs. Mamie Fielder Loses Control Of Car In Kentucky and Is Killed
BOMBS

While few people have the time
or interest to become genealogists,
you can preserve priceless segments of family history that might
otherwise be lost forever. Here you are encouraged to capture unique,
inspiring, or touching family stories that impart valuable life lessons.

It is essential that you begin recording whatever information you do have,
however sketchy or incomplete it might be. Begin with your family tree,
and follow by documenting useful information about
family medical history and any hereditary conditions.
Even one entry will expand your relatives' appreciation
and understanding of their ancestral origins.

To provide an added touch, you may wish to record family heritage
by interviewing relatives on video or audio tape. You may even
interview yourself. Many times this can help loved ones
through the grieving process. Be sure to record the locations
of the tapes and/or videos in the appropriate journal section.

Historical Family Stories

Tell us now about the colorful folks you call family, where they came from and what they did. The following pages are for you to record stories from family history involving parents, grandparents, siblings, or any other family member. Enter things as you would in a diary, adding bits here and there, and don't worry about the sequence or form.

_____
_____
_____
_____
_____
_____
_____
_____
_____
_____
_____
_____
_____
_____
_____

The Long Road Home

Your Living Legacy

Your Immediate Family Tree

_____   _____
         Your Name   married_____   Spouse
born _____ died _____   born _____ died _____

_____   _____
         Child #1   m_____   Spouse
     b _____ d _____   b _____ d _____

_____   _____   _____
    Grandchild #1   Grandchild #2   Grandchild #3
  b _____ d _____   b _____ d _____   b _____ d _____

_____   _____
         Child #2   m_____   Spouse
     b _____ d _____   b _____ d _____

_____   _____   _____
    Grandchild #1   Grandchild #2   Grandchild #3
  b _____ d _____   b _____ d _____   b _____ d _____

_____   _____
         Child #3   m_____   Spouse
     b _____ d _____   b _____ d _____

_____   _____   _____
    Grandchild #1   Grandchild #2   Grandchild #3
  b _____ d _____   b _____ d _____   b _____ d _____

Your Living Legacy

Your Extended Family Tree

_____   _____
          Stepchild #1   m_____   Spouse
      b _____ d _____   b _____ d _____

_____   _____   _____
Grandchild #1   Grandchild #2   Grandchild #3
b _____ d _____   b _____ d _____   b _____ d _____

_____   _____
          Stepchild #2   m_____   Spouse
      b _____ d _____   b _____ d _____

_____   _____   _____
Grandchild #1   Grandchild #2   Grandchild #3
b _____ d _____   b _____ d _____   b _____ d _____

_____   _____
          Stepchild #3   m_____   Spouse
      b _____ d   b _____ d _____

_____   _____   _____
Grandchild #1   Grandchild #2   Grandchild #3
b _____ d _____   b _____ d _____   b _____ d _____

The Long Road Home

Your Ancestors' Family Tree

_____ _____   _____ _____
Grandfather   Grandmother   Grandfather   Grandmother
     m_____   m_____
b____ d____ b____ d____   b____ d____ b____ d____

_____   _____
         Father   Mother
   b_____ d_____   b_____ d_____

_____   _____
        Sibling   Sibling
   b_____ d_____   b_____ d_____

_____   _____
        Sibling   Sibling
   b_____ d_____   b_____ d_____

_____   _____
        Sibling   Sibling
   b_____ d_____   b_____ d_____

_____
          Your Name
      b_____ d_____

_____
           Sibling
      b_____ d_____

_____
           Sibling
      b_____ d_____

Your Living Legacy

Family Medical History

Use this page to record hereditary family diseases such as diabetes, cancer, or heart disease.

Example:

Relative <u>Aunt Dorothy (grandmother's sister)</u>   Disease <u>Diabetes</u>

Diagnosed at age <u>59</u>   Cause of death <u>yes</u>   Age at death <u>77</u>

Comments <u>Aunt Dorothy was diagnosed early and kept to her exercise and diet,</u>
<u>which contributed to her living so many more years.</u>

Relative _____   Disease _____

Diagnosed at age _____ Cause of death _____ Age at death _____

Comments_____

_____

Relative _____   Disease _____

Diagnosed at age _____ Cause of death _____ Age at death _____

Comments_____

_____

Relative _____   Disease _____

Diagnosed at age _____ Cause of death _____ Age at death _____

Comments_____

_____

Relative _____   Disease _____

Diagnosed at age _____ Cause of death _____ Age at death _____

Comments_____

_____

List the details of any other family health issues, such as allergies, alcoholism, or depression, of which your relatives should be aware.

Location of Family Memorabilia

Some of the previous information in this chapter may have already been compiled in a family Bible, scrapbooks, letters, or other locations. Please use this page to tell relatives where this information can be found.

Example:

There is a shoe box in my bedroom closet labeled "letters" containing old letters Dad sent to Mother while they were dating and shortly before their marriage. Auntie June has family letters that were loaned to her many years ago.

_____
_____
_____
_____
_____
_____
_____
_____
_____
_____
_____
_____
_____

The Long Road Home

Chapter V

Exit Dancing
My Final Arrangements

All our lives we make big plans. We plan for the weather, the weekend, for weddings, for timetables and schedules, meetings and deadlines. We adjust our clocks, adjust the thermostat, adjust our attitudes. We hurry to make it across town, keep appointments, arrive late and leave early. We set the alarm, set the table, and upset each other. Our families help us and hurt us, then help us again. We count our blessings, count our change, and count to ten. We fill the gas tank, fill out forms, fill our wineglass. We make money, we make love, and we make amends. We break the rules and break our word, pick up the pieces and begin again. We pay the bills, pay our dues, and pay the piper.

The schedule life holds for most is in and out, up and down, back and forth. Day in and day out, the seconds become minutes; the minutes, hours; the hours pass into weeks; into years; into decades. Suddenly, overnight, we have done what would have taken a lifetime to achieve. We are grown up now—responsible adults. When we look behind us, we see more than when we look ahead. How did the tables turn like this? At what point in the journey did we get closer to the end? We realize, all too slowly, we must prepare for winter in the seasons of our lives. And once again, we must make plans.

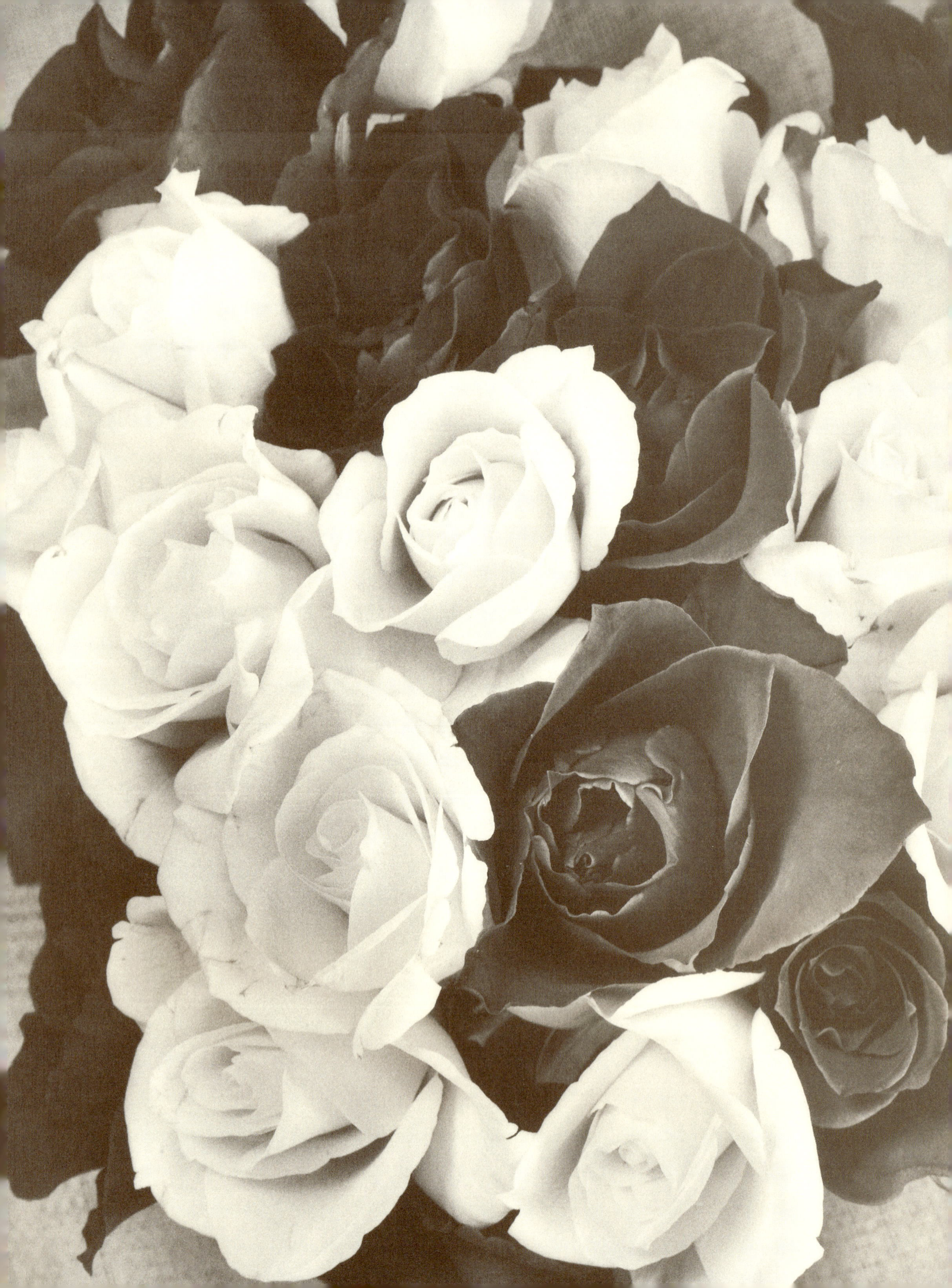

It is doubtful you would want to plan
one of life's most momentous occasions within 48 to 72 hours and
under intense emotional strain, with little or no idea of cost.
Yet, that's exactly what most of us leave our family to do
after we die. Rather than peace and resolution
for our survivors, funeral arrangements often breed chaos,
misgivings, and excessive expense.

Not only will writing down your memorial instructions
ensure the service you want; it will also guide your family in such
practical matters as type of casket and grave marker, burial instructions,
and desired expenditures. In turn, the last remembrances of
your presence on earth will evoke memories that bring
comfort to loved ones.

Don't Cry for Me

Do not stand at my grave and weep;
I am not here, I do not sleep.
I am a thousand winds that blow;
I am the diamond glints on snow.
I am the sunlight on ripened grain;
I am the gentle autumn's rain.

When you awaken in the morning's hush,
I am the swift uplifting rush
of quiet birds in circled flight.
I am the soft star that shines at night.
Do not stand at my grave and cry,
I am not here, I did not die.

—Author Unknown

Funeral-Memorial Arrangements

I would like _____
(name and phone number)
to be responsible for my funeral-memorial arrangements.

My preferences are as follows:

Funeral Home _____

Burial or Vault

Plot or Vault Location _____

Location of Plot/Vault Deed _____

Type of Vault _____

Type of Casket _____

Casket Color (outside/inside) _____ ☐ Open ☐ Closed

Type of Pall _____

Burial Attire _____

Jewelry _____

Hairstyle Instructions _____

Desired Hairstylist _____ Phone _____

Make-up Instructions _____

Desired Pallbearers

_____

_____

_____

Cremation

Ashes to be Interred at _____

By _____

Type of Urn _____

Disposition of Ashes _____

I would like my funeral-memorial to be:

☐ Open to all   ☐ Open only to family members and close friends

☐ Organized by my family   ☐ Other _____

I would like my funeral-memorial to be held at:

_____

_____

I would like _____ to conduct the service

Address _____ Phone _____

The following is a special poem, scripture, or quote that I have always held near to my heart. I would like it to be used in the remembrance card or printed program for my funeral service. (Specify if you want a photograph included in the program.)

_____

_____

_____

_____

I would like the following music (specify live music or tape):

_____
_____
_____

I would like the following poems, scriptures, or readings:

_____
_____
_____
_____
_____
_____

I would like the following people to speak, if willing:

_____
_____
_____

Special comments or requests:

_____
_____
_____
_____
_____
_____

I would like charitable donations in my memory sent to:

_____
_____

Other Arrangements

Funeral costs increase each year, so what you can afford now may be far less affordable in the future. Contact your insurance agent or preferred funeral home to set up a plan to cover the expenses of your funeral in advance.

The amount I would like to have budgeted for my funeral-memorial arrangements, including casket, is $ _____

☐ I have ☐ have not established a fund to cover my funeral expenses with

_____

_____

(Include address and phone number of insurance agent, funeral home, etc.)

Type of Memorial Marker _____

Epitaph _____

_____

I would like my Obituary Notice to include the following:

_____
_____
_____
_____
_____

I would like my Obituary Notice to be in the following newspapers:

_____
_____
_____
_____

The Voice of Experience

A very close friend sent me this letter when her mother died.
It punctuates the voice of experience.

Dear Susan,

This subject of death is so hard that I simply decided to write a letter to you telling you what my family and I have gone through.

The first decision that had to be made by me was the "pulling of the plug." Fortunately, Mom had a Durable Power of Attorney for Healthcare and a Living Will. She had stated to her doctor in previous meetings that she did not want life support systems beyond brain death. I think they only put her on the system at noon that day to give me time to get to Oklahoma and make my peace. After nine hours of watching her on that machine, its hideous, constant clanking, I gathered Janet and Rick and said it was time to give her some peace and quiet. Surrounding Mom with ourselves and our love, we watched the doctor remove the abusive tubes and sat with her in silence as she took in her last breath. As heartbreaking as it was, we felt a certain amount of strength because we had made the decision to let her go. That was 5:30 A.M., April 17.

By 9 A.M., the entire family was congregated at Mom's house. My uncles and Mary Ann were trying to make necessary lists for funeral arrangements. We were emotionally distraught, had been up all night, and were novices in this matter anyway. It would have been such a relief to go to a document and learn from Mom's own words just how she wanted her funeral to take place. The idea of one's own choice should play a big part in the funeral. The family has berths at the mausoleum and she was placed next to Dad, so we were spared that decision.

Our next trauma was picking a casket. We went top of the line with Mom and I don't to this day regret it. But once again, it can't be emphasized enough how easy this whole process would be if a document stating everything you want were there to be read. I almost feel it is a person's responsibility to provide guidelines for their own funeral for economic reasons.

Mom was buried on Saturday. We must have spent some portion of the next five days with the lawyers, gathering all of Mom's records for the IRS. The most important fact that I have to say about the decision of selecting an attorney is to establish a fee basis upfront by which he or she will be paid. Don't be afraid to ask and get a concrete answer on that price. You also have to like these people and have a good rapport with them as you will spend a lot of time with them over the next months, or as in our case, years.

It took us all summer and part of the fall to clear Mom's house of her things. I strongly suggest giving this process some time, meaning two or three months, before doing anything. Emotionally, it is draining. But at the same time, don't let too much time pass; it may become impossible to face. We had to prepare Mom's house for sale. Here again is a choice a person can and should make. Possessions should be securely labeled and set aside for people or dealt with in the deceased's own way.

Please bear with me. A lot of this stuff I'm still going through and it is very difficult to write about just now.

Love,
Carol

Vital Statistics
(May be required for Death Certificate)

Current Name _____

Name on Birth Certificate _____

Other Names During Your Life _____

Address _____

_____

Telephone No. _____

Years at Current Address _____

Current Occupation and Title _____

Past Occupations _____

_____

Current Business Address _____

_____

Business Telephone No. _____

Social Security No. _____

Veteran's Serial No. _____

Date of Birth _____

Place of Birth _____
(Hospital/Home, City, County, State, Country)

_____

Citizenship _____

Religious Affiliation _____

Spouse's Name _____

Spouse's Birthplace _____

Date and Place of Marriage _____

_____

Father's Complete Name _____

Father's Birthplace _____

Mother's Maiden Name _____

Mother's Complete Name _____

Mother's Birthplace _____

Professional Advisors

My trusted professional advisors are listed below for ease of contact.

Executor _____

Address _____

_____ Phone _____

Trustee of Estate _____

Address _____

_____ Phone _____

Attorney _____

Address _____

_____ Phone _____

Financial Advisor _____

Address _____

_____ Phone _____

Tax Advisor _____

Address _____

_____ Phone _____

Other _____

Address _____

_____ Phone _____

My preference for who should go through my personal belongings is:

Name _____ Phone _____

Relationship _____

Special Request(s) _____

My preference for who should go through my files at home is:

Name _____ Phone _____

Relationship _____

Special Request(s) _____

My preference for who should go through my files at the office is:

Name _____ Phone _____

Relationship _____

Special Request(s) _____

My preference for who should go through my safe deposit box is:

Name _____ Phone _____

Relationship _____

Special Request(s) _____

Consider this: All records that involve financial matters should be gone through by one person and the executor or trustee. Access to your safe deposit box requires one to be named on the signature card. After your death, your executor may also have access, but he or she will need proof of your death and his or her executorship.

For Your Information

In the event of my death, I would like to have:

Name _____ Phone _____

or alternatively, I would like to have:

Name _____ Phone _____

contact the following relatives, close friends, and neighbors:

Name _____ Home Phone _____
Relationship _____ Office Phone _____

Name _____ Home Phone _____
Relationship _____ Office Phone _____

Name _____ Home Phone _____
Relationship _____ Office Phone _____

Name _____ Home Phone _____
Relationship _____ Office Phone _____

Name _____ Home Phone _____
Relationship _____ Office Phone _____

Name _____ Home Phone _____
Relationship _____ Office Phone _____

Name _____ Home Phone _____
Relationship _____ Office Phone _____

Your Living Legacy

Others to contact

Religious Leader(s) _____ Phone _____

_____ Phone _____

_____ Phone _____

_____ Phone _____

Physician(s) _____ Phone _____

_____ Phone _____

_____ Phone _____

Dentist _____ Phone _____

Employer _____ Phone _____

Coworkers _____ Phone _____

_____ Phone _____

_____ Phone _____

_____ Phone _____

Others _____ Phone _____

_____ Phone _____

_____ Phone _____

_____ Phone _____

_____ Phone _____

_____ Phone _____

Others to be contacted may include your housekeeper, gardener, hairdresser, veterinarian, etc.

Professional Societies to Contact

Name_____ Phone _____

    Contact _____

Name_____ Phone _____

    Contact _____

Name_____ Phone _____

    Contact _____

Other Organizations to Contact

Name_____ Phone _____

    Contact _____

Name_____ Phone _____

    Contact _____

Name_____ Phone _____

    Contact _____

Name_____ Phone _____

    Contact _____

Volunteer Affiliations to Contact

Agency_____ Phone _____

    Contact _____

Agency_____ Phone _____

    Contact _____

Agency_____ Phone _____

    Contact _____

Personal Notes

Exit Dancing

Your Living Legacy

Chapter VI

Practical Issues
Getting Organized

I need to get organized, I think to myself. Behind hatboxes and shoeboxes, last year's styles, and tomorrow's dry cleaning, I reach into the darkness of my closet. The jewelry box has seen better days, its hinges worn and mirror broken. Inside, treasures lay wrapped in tissue. A dance card from junior high, its tiny pencil dangling from twisted string, a lonely heart wallflower left unattended. A letter from World War II includes a snapshot of some distant cousin twice removed. A broken necklace, a pressed pansy, a marriage license from 1894. I need to get organized, I think to myself. The same thought has crossed my mind for years, each time I have moved this jewelry box and its precious cargo. The contents reflect a simpler time, when a man's word and his handshake were all that was needed, where people called each other neighbor, and left their doors unlocked at night. This is not the case now. Life is complicated, all plastic cards and magnetic strips, digital display, secret codes, and button-pushing. I need to consider the practical issues of bank accounts and safe-deposit boxes, insurance policies and estate planning. My mind wanders as I slip onto my finger the soft gold band my father gave my mother. I need to get organized, I think to myself. I need to consider the practical issues.

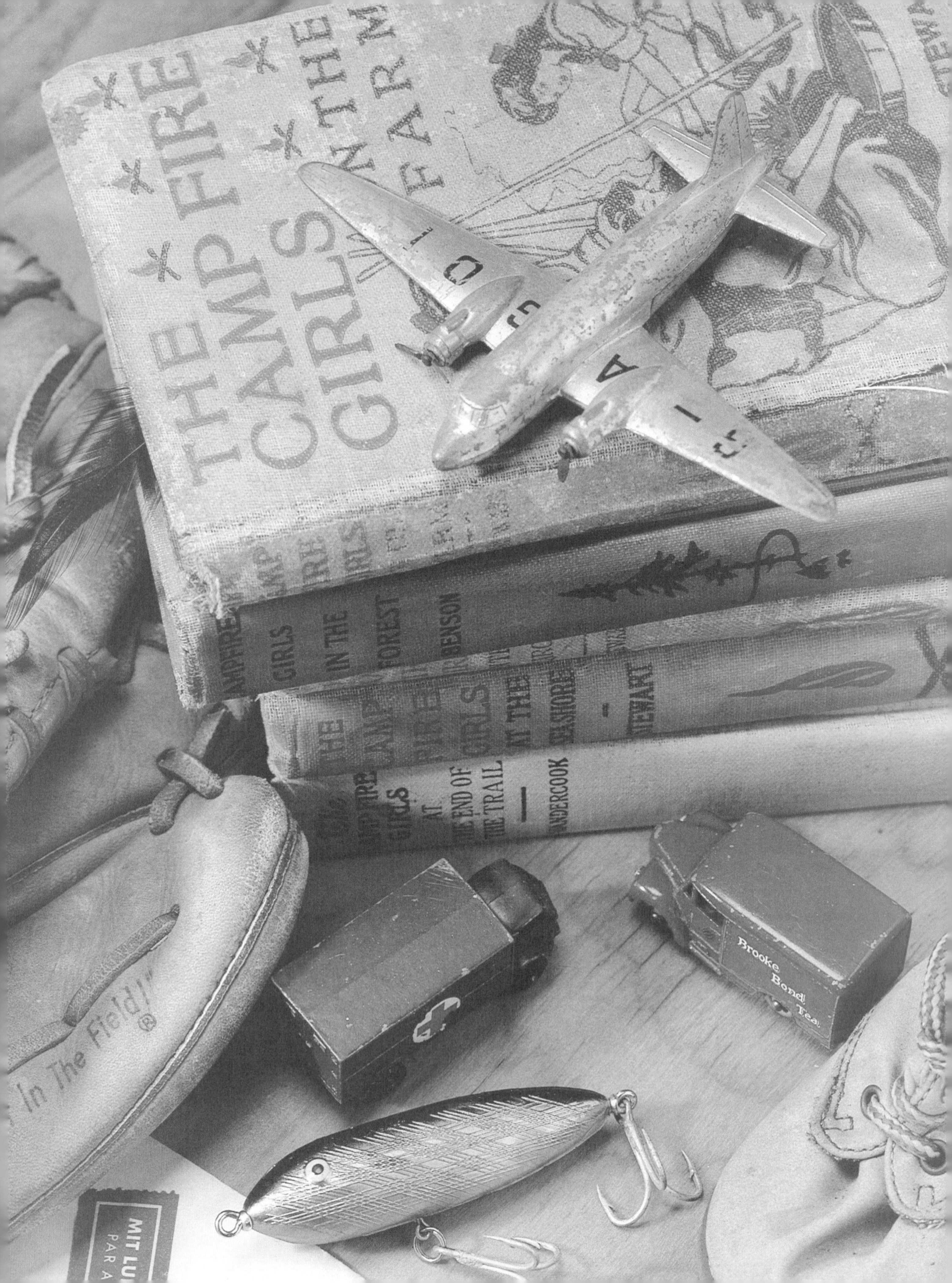
THE CAMP FIRE GIRLS
GIRLS IN THE FOREST
BENSON
STEWART
AT THE END OF THE TRAIL
VANDERCOOK
Brooke Bond Tea
In The Field!®

Practical Issues

Getting organized comes easier for some than others.

This chapter contains answers to common questions
regarding your estate, making a Will, choosing an executor,
and other considerations that will simplify the burden
of decision making for your family.
Included are examples of a Living Will
and organ donor forms, as well as valuable information
concerning Social Security and Veterans benefits.

Ease the trauma of your loved ones
by clearly guiding them to the pertinent information they will need.
On the following pages, identify the location, or a trusted confidant
who knows the location, of important documents, bank accounts,
passwords, insurance policies, deeds, and records.

Record of Important Documents, Etc.

Document Location/Trusted Confidant(s)

Certificates

    Birth _____

    Adoption _____

    Citizenship Papers _____

    Marriage _____

    Social Security Card _____

Ready Cash for Spouse _____

Will _____

Trust Agreements _____

  _____

Guardian Records for Minors _____

  _____

Living Will _____

Organ Donor Card _____

Power of Attorney Agreement _____

Military Service Records _____

Military Discharge Papers _____

Medical Records _____

  _____

Disability Claims _____

  _____

Diplomas _____

  _____

  _____

Practical Issues

Document   **Location/Trusted Confidant(s)**

Retirement/Pension Records   _____
                                _____

Investment Records   _____
                                _____
                                _____

Debt Records   _____
                                _____

Active Credit Cards   _____
                                _____
                                _____
                                _____

Bank Records   _____
                                _____
                                _____

Safe-Deposit Box   _____
Income Tax Returns   _____
Real Property Deeds   _____
                                _____

Titles (Cars, Boats, Etc.)   _____
                                _____
                                _____

Business Agreements   _____
                                _____
                                _____

Nuptial Agreements   _____
Divorce Decree   _____

Other   Location/Trusted Confidant(s)

Safe-Deposit Box Key   _____
Home Keys   _____
Car Keys   _____
File Keys   _____
Extra Keys   _____
Security PIN Numbers   _____
                        _____
                        _____

Combination Lock Numbers _____
Computer Files   _____
Computer Passwords   _____
Manuals   _____
Warranties   _____

Special Operation Instructions

_____
_____
_____

Other Miscellaneous Items

_____
_____
_____
_____
_____
_____

For added assurance, have extra copies of important documents accessible to one or more trusted confidant(s). Keep these copies in a safe place in your home, such as a fireproof box, and store a copy in your safe-deposit box.

Practical Issues

The Voice of Experience

A special friend who lost her sister wanted to share her experience.

Susan,

You need to identify who is responsible for filing insurance claims. If someone has been ill for a long time with institutional care, the unfiled claims could go back for years. My sister was just too ill to file claims for as far back as two years. She paid thousands for medicines that were not claimed on her insurance. She also had tests and procedures for which I filed claims that paid thousands to us.

Often people have cancer policies that do not pay an institution but pay directly to the insured. Therefore, no institution will file for you. I was unaware that my sister had such a policy, but after finding some papers, I investigated and filed them, which in my sister's case resulted in a significant payment to her estate.

I consider insurance a very big issue as it is very time-consuming and confusing. I spent about three months locating items, getting proper documentation, and filing claims. Also, it can be one of the most valuable gifts you leave in your estate.

Vivian

Insurance Records

Life Insurance

Company _____ Beneficiary _____

Location of Policy _____

Company _____ Beneficiary _____

Location of Policy _____

Company _____ Beneficiary _____

Location of Policy _____

Pensions/Annuities

Company _____ Beneficiary _____

Location of Contract _____

Company _____ Beneficiary _____

Location of Contract _____

Company _____ Beneficiary _____

Location of Contract _____

Other

Company/Type _____

Location _____

Other Items/Documents

Item or Document _____

Location _____

Item or Document _____

Location _____

Item or Document _____

Location _____

Item or Document _____

Location _____

Item or Document _____

Location _____

Item or Document _____

Location _____

Item or Document _____

Location _____

Item or Document _____

Location _____

Item or Document _____

Location _____

Item or Document _____

Location _____

Item or Document _____

Location _____

Your Will

A Will is a plan for your financial affairs after you depart, but it also brings peace of mind while you are living. It is a document that explains what will happen to the things you own, who will care for your minor children, and who will serve as executor to settle your affairs. It is your guarantee that important decisions you made in your lifetime will be carried out according to your wishes.

What will happen if you don't have a Will?

Laws can vary from state to state, but one thing is guaranteed: someone else will decide how to distribute your estate. Only relatives are allowed to inherit if you die without a Will. This means your friends, former spouse, or favorite charity would receive nothing. If there are no living relatives, it can all be passed to the state. If you have a fiancé(e) or close friend, they will receive nothing.

What is an estate?

Anything you own constitutes your estate. That includes bank accounts, stocks, cars, jewelry, real estate, businesses, coin collections, or art collections. Your Will determines what specific items will be left to certain individuals.

Wills seldom deal with the distribution of personal belongings as addressed in this workbook. Accordingly, the information herein is an informal supplement to your Will. In any event, sharing this workbook with your Will originator, your executor, or a trusted confidant will help communicate your full intentions.

What property is not covered by a Will?

Specific types of property are not covered by a Will:

- Life insurance and retirement plans that designate individuals or any entity other than the deceased's estate as the beneficiary are not covered by a Will.

- Property you have placed in a Living Trust during your lifetime goes to the trust's beneficiaries.

- Property you have owned as joint tenant will automatically be inherited by the co-owner(s).

In certain states, the money, real estate, and possessions you and your spouse acquire during your marriage are considered community property. If one spouse earns more than another, the property is still equal in distribution. Your Will can affect only your half of the community property.

Be sure your Will is kept current and that your executor or confidant knows its location.

Your Executor

When selecting an executor, it is most important to remember that the person you leave in charge of your affairs can no longer turn to you for advice, leaving the decisions regarding your estate totally in his or her hands. Many of these questions are simply matters of taste or preference, while others require expert knowledge of tax law. An appropriate executor is a person who is totally trustworthy and knows your beneficiaries. For every beneficiary there will be a different point of view as to your intentions.

The attitude "I'll be long gone, let someone else worry about who gets what" is very shortsighted when talking about those who love you. A perfect example is the husband who has always taken full financial responsibility for his family. The wife receives an allowance for household needs, without any worry as to from where the money comes. When the husband dies suddenly, she is made the executor of the estate. This can be an overwhelming task to someone who has never had to balance a checkbook. Make a conscientious choice. Do not ask more of your loved ones after your death than you would have in life.

Periodically, be sure to take your executor and main beneficiary through your home, pointing out personal belongings with special memories and intentions. Sharing this book with them before you die will be the closest you get to being at the reading of your own Will. Help them out. Be their guide through this ordeal. It will lighten their emotional burden, and you can rest knowing your wishes will be accomplished.

Practical Issues

Your Living Will

If you desire to entrust your life's wishes to a loved one in the event you become totally disabled, you need a Living Will.

Following is an example of a Living Will:

Living Will

To my family, physician, lawyer, and clergy:

To any medical facility in whose care I happen to be:

To any individual who may become responsible for my health, welfare, or affairs:

I wish to make this statement as an expression of my desires while I am still of sound and competent mind. If a time comes when I can no longer take part in decisions regarding my own well-being, let this statement serve as a guide to all those who care for me.

Should a situation arise when there is no reasonable expectation of my recovering from extreme physical or mental disability, I request that I be allowed to die and not be kept alive by artificial means or "heroic measures" undertaken by medical personnel. I do, however, ask that medication be mercifully administered to me to alleviate pain and suffering even though this may hasten the moment of death.

If I have executed a valid form of bequeathal of any of my organs for transplant or research purposes, I do ask and authorize that I be kept alive by artificial means for a time sufficient to enable the medical personnel to accomplish the withdrawal of the organs.

I am making this request after careful consideration and it is in accordance with my beliefs and convictions. I hope that those who care for me will feel morally bound to carry out my wishes as expressed here.

Signature _____ Date _____

Witness _____

Witness _____

Witness _____

Living Wills are different from state to state. A letter from you will not be honored by law. Overall, a Living Will states that if there is no hope and your death is imminent, you do not wish to be kept alive by artificial means.

You must use the form from your own state.

Your Living Legacy

Organ Donation

Donation of your body or specific organs should not be a part of your Will for the simple reason that it's often discovered too late to honor your wishes. Make sure your doctor and your family have copies of the appropriate form.

Following is an example of a Uniform Donor Card:

A Uniform Donor Card

of _____
(Print or type name of donor)

In the hope that I may help others, I hereby make this anatomical gift, if medically acceptable, to take effect upon my death. The words and marks below indicate my desires.

I give: (a) any needed or physical parts.

(b) only the following organs or physical parts:

_____
(specify organs or physical parts)
for the purpose of transplantation, therapy, medical research or education.

(c) my body for anatomical study if needed.

Limitations or special wishes, if any:

Signed by the donor and the following two witnesses in the presence of each other:

Signature of donor _____   *Birthdate of donor* _____

Date signed _____   *City and State* _____

Witness _____   *Witness* _____

Similar to Living Wills, Organ Donor forms vary from state to state.

You must use the form from your own state.

Social Security Benefits

Social Security is a form of insurance that should be attended to after any death. Most of us are entitled to some form of these benefits. But it is important to realize that Social Security benefits are not paid automatically. One must apply for these benefits on special forms, and certain documents must be furnished at that time. The forms and documents listed below must be furnished within a specific time limit.

- Certified Copy of Death Certificate
- Social Security Card or Number
- Copy of Marriage Certificate
- Birth Certificate of Applicant
- Birth Certificate of Deceased
- Birth Certificates of Minor Children
- Disability Proof for Children over 18
- Receipted Funeral Bill
  (if applicant is other than the surviving spouse)
- Proof of Support if Applicant is Parent or Husband.

As appropriate, designate the location of these documents in the earlier section of this chapter. You may wish to asterisk the documents relevant to obtaining Social Security benefits for your family.

Contact your local Social Security Office for current information on benefits and claims procedures, or call (800) 772-1213.

Veterans Benefits

Survivors of veterans are entitled to many burial-related benefits. However, these benefits will not be paid automatically. Claims for Veterans benefits must be made within certain prescribed time limits.

As an honorably discharged veteran from the Air Force, Army, Navy, Marine Corps, or Coast Guard, you may be entitled to the following:

- A burial allowance limited to $300 for expenses for burial and funeral of the deceased. This allowance will be paid only for veterans who were entitled to receive a Veterans Administration pension or compensation.

- A limited allowance for burial and funeral expenses of the deceased.

- A burial flag, that can be given to the next of kin or friend of the deceased.

- A bronze memorial or granite grave marker.

To have your claim filed, the following forms may be required:
- Veterans Discharge Papers
- Certified Copy of Death Certificate
- Copy of Marriage Certificate
- Birth Certificate of Minor Children
- Receipted Itemized Funeral Bill

As appropriate, designate the location of these documents in the earlier section of this chapter. As with the documents needed for obtaining Social Security benefits, you may wish to asterisk such documents for ease of obtaining family benefits.

Veterans benefits are frequently altered and revised. There may also be Veterans benefits from your county. To determine your eligibility or to file your claim, contact your local Veterans Affairs office or call (800) 827-1000.

Personal Thoughts & Reflections

Use these pages for any additional entries you may wish to include.

Your Living Legacy

Practical Issues

Sands of Time

In the stillness of the night, I travel to familiar places in my mind. The grandfather clock ticks a steady heartbeat through the hushed quiet, and I am comforted by its sound. Like hearing the footsteps of a parent down a long hallway, I feel safe. I know this clock has seen generations of my family, though where it stands has changed often. Some things do not change: we are born, we learn to rise after falling down, we laugh in the middle of our tears, and we hope love will find us on our journey. Always too soon, it seems, we die. This scenario can be short or long, bittersweet or joy-filled, riddled with angst or iced with excitement, but generally it is like a wave upon the sand, ever lapping at the shore in a rhythm all its own. We can neither start nor stop it, only interrupt it with our presence, and appreciate it while we're there. Like my grandfather clock, my face, too, has grown older, but each hour still chimes, and I realize how grateful I am to have been a particle in the sands of time.

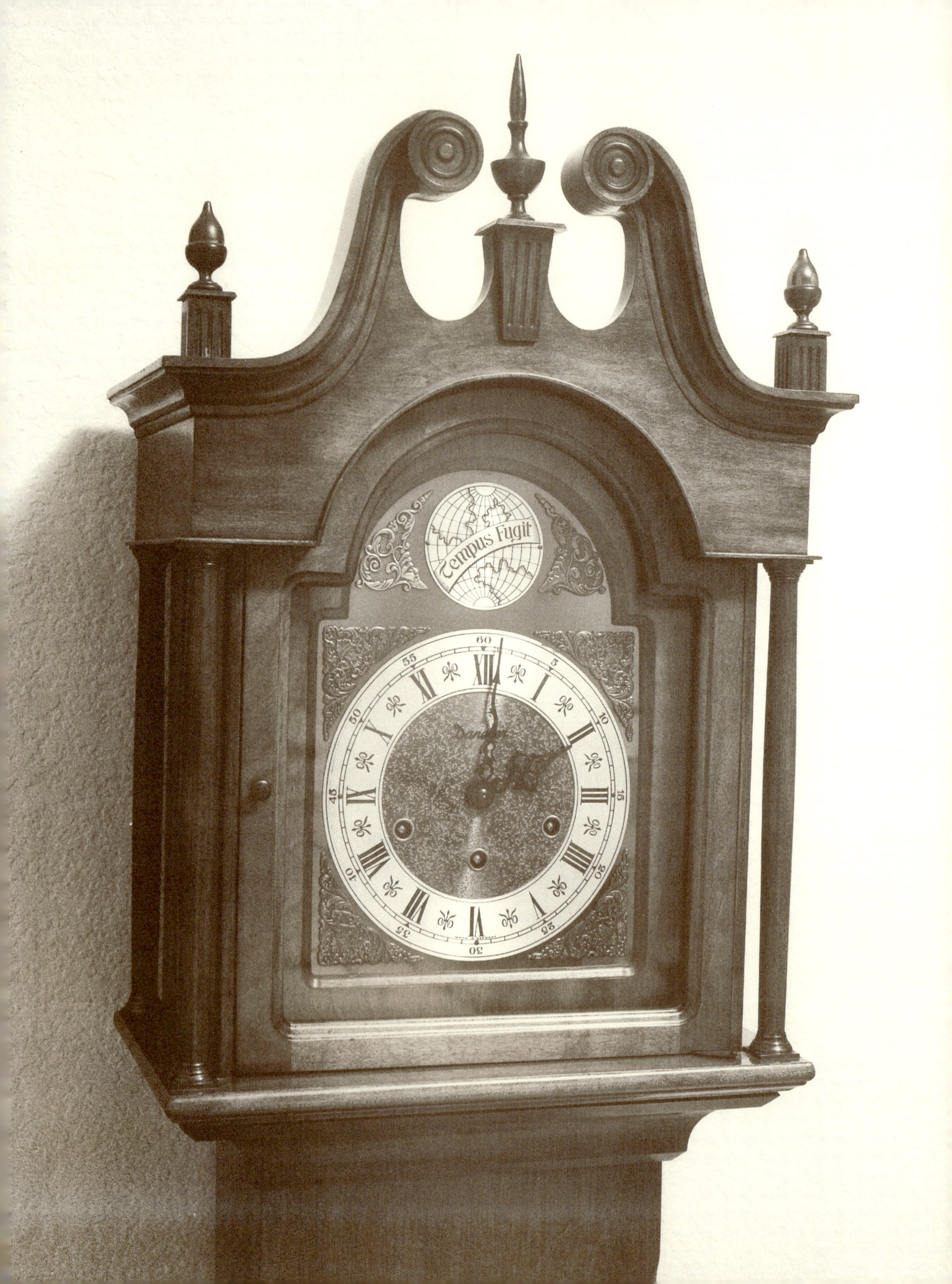
Tempus Fugit

Sands of Time

For convenience in contacting loved ones who have received
special thoughts or gifts herein, list their names and addresses below.

Name _____ Relationship _____ Phone _____
Address _____
Name _____ Relationship _____ Phone _____
Address _____
Name _____ Relationship _____ Phone _____
Address _____
Name _____ Relationship _____ Phone _____
Address _____
Name _____ Relationship _____ Phone _____
Address _____
Name _____ Relationship _____ Phone _____
Address _____
Name _____ Relationship _____ Phone _____
Address _____
Name _____ Relationship _____ Phone _____
Address _____
Name _____ Relationship _____ Phone _____
Address _____
Name _____ Relationship _____ Phone _____
Address _____

Name	Relationship	Phone
Address		
Name	Relationship	Phone
Address		
Name	Relationship	Phone
Address		
Name	Relationship	Phone
Address		
Name	Relationship	Phone
Address		
Name	Relationship	Phone
Address		
Name	Relationship	Phone
Address		
Name	Relationship	Phone
Address		
Name	Relationship	Phone
Address		
Name	Relationship	Phone
Address		
Name	Relationship	Phone
Address		

Sands of Time

Name _____ Relationship _____ Phone _____
Address _____

Name _____ Relationship _____ Phone _____
Address _____

Name _____ Relationship _____ Phone _____
Address _____

Name _____ Relationship _____ Phone _____
Address _____

Name _____ Relationship _____ Phone _____
Address _____

Name _____ Relationship _____ Phone _____
Address _____

Name _____ Relationship _____ Phone _____
Address _____

Name _____ Relationship _____ Phone _____
Address _____

Name _____ Relationship _____ Phone _____
Address _____

Name _____ Relationship _____ Phone _____
Address _____

About the Author

Susan Fielder Mears lives in Del Mar, California, with her husband, Dan, and Hooter, their Moluccan Cockatoo. A businesswoman and owner, entrepreneur, entertainer, and fund-raiser, her interests and talents are many and varied. In loving memory, this book is dedicated to her mother, Guynelle, her grandmother, Vivian, and a very special little girl named Jennifer, who lost her battle with leukemia. Susan was named Woman of the Year by Brooks Brothers in 1993 for her fund-raising efforts in support of the Leukemia Society. For this, Susan and Jennifer graced San Diego billboards. She also recently received the 1997 *San Diego Business Journal* Women in Business Award in marketing. Susan has thoughtfully created this book as a labor of love to assist others in documenting a personal journal to guide loved ones.